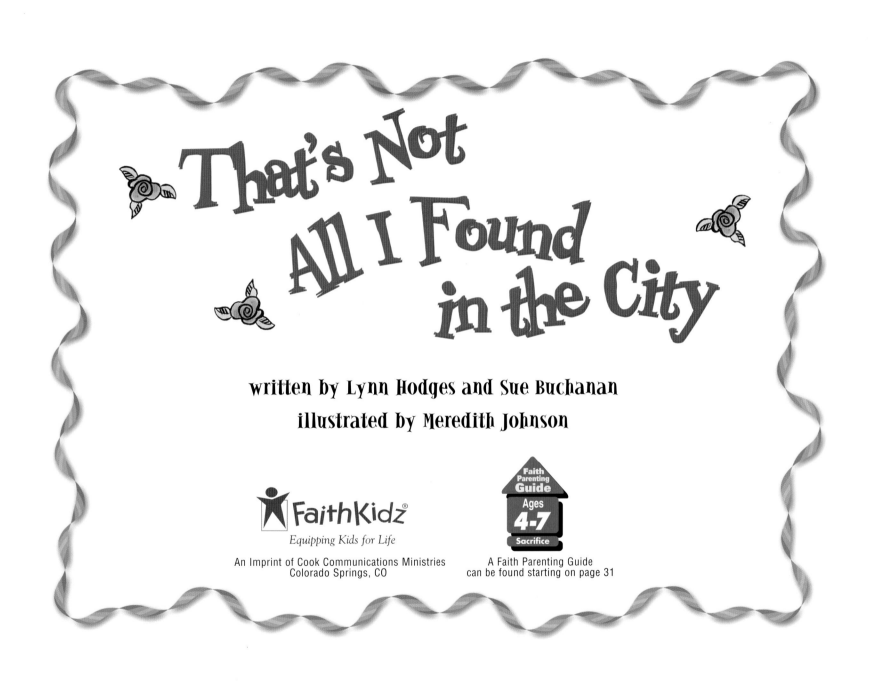

That's Not All I Found in the City

written by Lynn Hodges and Sue Buchanan

illustrated by Meredith Johnson

FaithKidz®
Equipping Kids for Life

An Imprint of Cook Communications Ministries
Colorado Springs, CO

Faith Parenting Guide
Ages **4-7**
Sacrifice

A Faith Parenting Guide
can be found starting on page 31

Faith Kidz® is an imprint of Cook Communications Ministries
Colorado Springs, Colorado 80918
Cook Communications, Paris, Ontario
Kingsway Communications, Eastbourne, England

First printing, 2005
Printed in China
1 2 3 4 5 6 7 8 9 10 Printing/Year 09 08 07 06 05

ISBN 0781441641

Editor: Heather Gemmen
Creative Director: Randy Maid
Interior Design Manager: Nancy L. Haskins
Interior Designer: Helen H. Harrison
Cover Design Manager: Jeffrey P. Barnes

Dedication

To my children:
Nathan, Libby, and Mary Peyton.
You contagiously live life to the fullest and
consistently exemplify your Christian walk.
–L.H.

For the best friends a girl could have:
Janet, Carlene, and Susie.
We found each other in high school
and never let go.
– S.B.

Ashton! Debbie! Keep it down! There are people in this hotel who want to sleep!"

"Oh, Mrs. Danbury, I'm sorry. I'm just so excited to be in New York City!" replied Debbie. "I've never been anywhere, except in books."

"You've been places in books?" Ashton asked.

"Well, my mom and I read about airplanes and taxis and faraway places. We even read about a girl who lived in a hotel. But now I get to see it all for myself!

Oh, Mrs. Danbury, thank you so much! And thank you for taking us shopping! My Easter dress is the most beautiful dress I've ever had!"

shton leaped off the bed and into the conversation. "And thank you for taking us to that famous ice cream shop for frozen hot chocolate and—"

"to the candy store…" Debbie added.

"…with the peppermint stools!"

"And the humongous candy bars!"

"Girls!" Mrs. Danbury warned, laughing. "Keep it down!"

I felt like Willy Wonka!" Debbie said in a softer voice. "Remember that book, Ashton? It's about a boy who goes to a—"

"I saw the movie!" interrupted Ashton. "Movies are way better."

"My mom says that books free your imagination."

W here does your mom get all these books?" Ashton asked.

"She goes to the library once a week. My dad says he would go for her. You know how sick she is. But Mom knows which books I'll love best, and so she never misses a week."

No wonder you never go anywhere. All you do is read!" Ashton said.

"Well, now I'm someplace!" Debbie answered. "And I want to find every single place my mom told me about!"

And I want to find every single shop in the city," sighed Ashton. "I want to buy the perfect thing to remind me of New York."

The next morning the girls were up early. "Can we please wear our new Easter dresses, Mom?" Ashton begged.

"It's not quite Easter yet, but it's okay with me."

After breakfast, the hotel doorman blew a whistle—startling Debbie and triggering giggles in the girls. A cab lurched to the curb, and off they went to Times Square.

But that was just the beginning. They saw St. Patrick's Cathedral, the United Nations Building, the Empire State Building, China Town, the Statue of Liberty and…

Rockefeller Center!" Debbie cried. "My mom showed me this place!"

"She did?" Ashton asked.
"Yep. In a book."

14

They had lunch in a part of town called the Fulton Fish Market, where they sat at outdoor tables. Jugglers and mimes kept them laughing as they ate. One very silly clown on a huge unicycle came right toward them and would have landed in their lunch had he not jerked his bike in the other direction at the very last minute.

A shton," Mrs. Danbury whispered to the girls as they slipped onto the subway that would take them to Central Park, "should we tell Debbie about her surprise?"

"O h, tell me! Please tell me!" Debbie begged as the train bumped and jerked along the track. But just at that moment the lights flickered and Debbie squealed. "What's happening?"

"Don't worry, Debbie," Ashton assured her. "We'll come back up to see the sunlight soon. And then you'll have your surprise."

Skipping up the stairs a step ahead of her friend, Debbie couldn't stop smiling. She drew her breath when she saw the horse-drawn carriage covered with roses.

"It's for us," Ashton told her. "It's your surprise."

"Wow!" Debbie whispered. "I feel like Cinderella!" She climbed into the beautiful carriage. "All I need are glass slippers!"

xcept for the clop, clop of the horse's feet and the squeak of the carriage, it was quiet as they looked around at the beautiful, tree-filled park.

"My mom and I have read about so many of the places we've been today," mused Debbie. "Everything is just as exciting as I imagined it."

Mrs. Danbury put an arm around Debbie's shoulder. "Yes, but I hope you know that a pretty dress and a fun vacation are nothing compared to what your mom has given you. She has given you so much more."

Just as they rounded the corner next to a huge building with banners flying across the front, they felt a drop.

"Uh, oh," said Mrs. Danbury. "Rain!"

"Where did that come from?" Ashton asked.

"Come on, girls! Run for it!"

"I'm ruined!" Ashton exclaimed. "I need a hair dryer."

"No hair dryers here," answered Debbie. "It's the Metropolitan Museum of Art. My mom—"

"Wait! Let me guess. Your mom and you read all about it!"

Debbie smiled. "Yeah, we did. I guess I've been a lot more places than I thought."

They slowly made their way through the exhibits. Ashton looked around in awe. "Look at this fancy furniture," she whispered. "And the fancy jewelry … and all the fancy gold and silver coins. And I especially love those fancy stained-glass windows. I love this place!"

"Those windows have been around for hundreds of years," Mrs. Danbury explained.

C"an we see the Tiffany windows?" Debbie asked. "I know they are here someplace. My mom and I—"

"—read about it in a book!" Ashton finished for her.

"Yep!" Debbie responded with a laugh.

The three quickly found the Louis Comfort Tiffany exhibit. There were large mosaics, beautiful vases, and gorgeous lamps. There was jewelry and—Ashton's favorite—large windows of stained glass. Ashton couldn't hide her opinion: "Faaan-ceey!"

As they turned a corner, Debbie let out a too-loud-for-a-museum whoop, followed by a "shush" from the security guard standing nearby.

"Dogwood!" Debbie gushed. "That's one of the things I wanted to find. Do you know what my mom told me?" Debbie didn't wait for an answer. "She read a legend about the dogwood tree—that the petals can remind us of Jesus' death. Look at the blossoms—each one is the shape of a cross. If you look real close, you can see a dark red stain on the tips of the petals. That represents the bloodstains. The center looks like a thorny crown. It's sym ... sym ... bolic."

Debbie explained more. "Every year at Easter we watch for our dogwood tree to spring to life—to remind us of how Jesus came to back to life. Then we pick a huge bouquet for our table, and my dad reads the Easter story—about how Jesus gave his life for us, how he rose from the dead so we can live forever."

"Jesus gave us so much more than fun vacations or even exciting books to read, didn't he?" Mrs. Danbury prompted quietly.

C ome on," Ashton urged. "Let's go find something cool in the gift store." As Ashton scampered off, Debbie looked at Mrs. Danbury and smiled. "I think I just found the very best gift of all."

In the museum store, Debbie picked out a lovely ornament of the Tiffany dogwood to hang in her mother's window.

And Ashton chose (who would have dreamed?)…

… a book!

That's Not All I Found in the City

Life Issue: **I want my children to understand the sacrifice Jesus made when he died on the cross for our sins.**
Spiritual Building Block: **Sacrifice**

Do the following activities to help your children understand the sacrifice Jesus made for us at Easter.

Sight:

Take your children to an exhibit, gallery, or museum to experience fine art firsthand. Or visit a library to find books depicting great works of art. Ask your children to describe what they find beautiful, fascinating, or unique about what the artists created. Then discuss together: How is God like an artist? Where do you see God's "artwork" in what he created? Look for art examples that depict Jesus—his life on earth, his death, and his resurrection. Talk together about what Jesus sacrificed to be our Savior: What did Jesus give up to come here? Why did he do it? What sacrifices can we make as a reflection of the sacrifice he made for us at Easter?

That's Not All I Found in the City

Life Issue: **I want my children to understand the sacrifice Jesus made when he died on the cross for our sins.**
Spiritual Building Block: **Sacrifice**

Do the following activities to help your children understand the sacrifice Jesus made for us at Easter.

Sound:

With your children, play CDs or listen to radio stations that demonstrate music from different cultures. Discuss why God gave us music and how God loves people of every culture. If possible, listen to worship music from other cultures or languages and talk about how each kind expresses unique praise to the Lord. Then use music to thank Jesus for his sacrifice on the cross—you and your children could sing along with a recording or make up your own praise songs to God.

That's Not All I Found in the City

Life Issue: **I want my children to understand the sacrifice Jesus made when he died on the cross for our sins.**
Spiritual Building Block: **Sacrifice**

Do the following activities to help your children understand the sacrifice Jesus made for us at Easter.

Touch:

Find a safe spot to have a good, old-fashioned pillow fight with your family. Encourage fun and discourage competition. Then settle down in a pile of pillows to talk about how peaceful and comforting they can make us feel. Talk together about the comfort and peace we can receive from our heavenly Father because of Jesus' sacrifice on the cross. Read the crucifixion and resurrection account from one of the Gospels (Matthew 27–28; Mark 15–16; Luke 23–24; John 19–20). Pray together to thank Jesus for his sacrifice—and for the wonderful friendship we can have with him because of what he did for us.

The Word at Work Around the World

What would you do if you wanted to share God's love with children on the streets of your city? That's the dilemma David C. Cook faced in 1870's Chicago. His answer was to create literature that would capture children's hearts.

Out of those humble beginnings grew a worldwide ministry that has used literature to proclaim God's love and disciple generation after generation. Cook Communications Ministries is committed to personal discipleship—to helping people of all ages learn God's Word, embrace His salvation, walk in His ways, and minister in His name.

Faith Kidz, RiverOak, Honor, Life Journey, Victor, NextGen . . . every time you purchase a book produced by Cook Communications Ministries, you not only meet a vital personal need in your life or in the life of someone you love, but you're also a part of ministering to José in Colombia, Humberto in Chile, Gousa in India, or Lidiane in Brazil. You help make it possible for a pastor in China, a child in Peru, or a mother in West Africa to enjoy a life-changing book. And because you helped, children and adults around the world are learning God's Word and walking in His ways.

Thank you for your partnership in helping to disciple the world. May God bless you with the power of His Word in your life.

For more information about our international ministries, visit www.ccmi.org.

Additional copies of this book are available from your local bookstore.

If you have enjoyed this book, or if it has impacted your life, we would like to hear from you.

Please contact us at:
Cook Communications Ministries
4050 Lee Vance View
Colorado Springs, CO 80918
www.cookministries.com